Special thanks to our adviser:
Susan Kesselring, M.A., Literacy Educator
Rosemount—Apple Valley—Eagan (Minnesota) School District

One President Was Born on Independence Day

and Other **Freaky Facts** About the **26**th Through **43**rd Presidents

by **Barbara Seuling**
illustrated by **Matthew Skeens**

PiCTURE WiNDOW BOOKS
Minneapolis, Minnesota

Editor: Christianne Jones
Designer: Abbey Fitzgerald
Page Production: Michelle Biedscheid
Art Director: Nathan Gassman
The illustrations in this book were created digitally.

Picture Window Books
5115 Excelsior Boulevard
Suite 232
Minneapolis, MN 55416
877-845-8392
www.picturewindowbooks.com

Printed in the United States of America.

Library of Congress Cataloging-in-Publication Data
Seuling, Barbara.
One president was born on Independence Day : and other freaky
facts about the 26th Through 43rd presidents / by Barbara
Seuling ; illustrated by Matthew Skeens.
p. cm. — (Freaky facts)
Includes bibliographical references and index.
ISBN 978-1-4048-4118-5 (library binding)
1. Presidents—United States—Biography—Miscellanea—
Juvenile literature. 2. Presidents—United States—History—
20th century—Miscellanea—Juvenile literature. 3. Presidents—
United States—History—21st century—Miscellanea—Juvenile
literature. I. Skeens, Matthew. II. Title.
E176.1.S495 2008
973.09'9—dc22   2007032918

Table of Contents

Theodore Roosevelt
(1901-1909)

Rumor has it that Theodore Roosevelt had the West Wing added to the White House so he could have some privacy from his six children.

Roosevelt was the 25th person to hold the job of president, but he is called the 26th president. That's because Grover Cleveland was president two separate times. Cleveland counts as the 22nd president and 24th president. He served from 1885 to 1889 and from 1893 to 1897. William McKinley became president in 1897, and after his death in 1901, Roosevelt took over the job.

Roosevelt was the first president to leave the United States while in office. In 1906, he visited the site of the Panama Canal.

4

William Howard Taft
(1909-1913)

William Howard Taft had a reputation for falling asleep in conferences, while signing papers, sitting for his portrait—anywhere at anytime. Once, he fell asleep at a funeral.

Taft weighed more than 300 pounds (135 kg). A special bathtub had to be built for him.

Taft was the first president to throw out the first pitch at the opening of the baseball season. The White House had his box at the ballpark equipped with a special oversized chair to fit him.

Taft was the last president to have a moustache.

(1913-1921)

A tobacco-chewing ram and 20 sheep roamed the White House lawns during Wilson's administration. The wool from the sheep was sold and raised more than $100,000 for the Red Cross.

The president's given name was Thomas Woodrow Wilson. As a child, he was called Tommy. Later, as a professor, Wilson thought Woodrow sounded more dignified. He was known for the rest of his life as Woodrow.

President Wilson could not read properly until he was 9 years old. Until then, he read everything backward. It is now clear that he had dyslexia.

Before Wilson was president of the United States, he was the president of Princeton University from 1902–1910.

Woodrow Wilson did not have an inaugural ball. He thought the ball was inappropriate for such a serious occasion.

Wilson was the first president to hold regular White House press conferences.

Wilson enjoyed playing bridge, golfing, swimming, and horseback riding.

Wilson and his first wife, Ellen, exchanged more than 1,000 love notes in their 28 years of marriage. Ellen died of a liver condition, at the age of 54, in 1914.

When President Wilson suffered a stroke, his second wife, Edith, would not let anyone see him without getting her approval. Edith was sometimes called the first woman president because many people believed that she made all of the decisions while Wilson was sick.

In 1920, President Wilson was awarded the Nobel Peace Prize for his peace-making efforts during World War I (1914–1918).

Warren G. Harding
(1921-1923)

At 19, Warren G. Harding ran a newspaper in Marion, Ohio. After his inauguration, he went back to Marion and stopped at his old newspaper office. He rolled up his sleeves and helped produce the newspaper.

Harding was the first president for whom women could vote.

To get in shape for his presidential campaign, Harding played pingpong every morning, tennis every afternoon, and golf a couple of times each week.

Harding was the first president to ride to his inauguration in an automobile.

President Harding's inaugural address lasted 37 minutes. It was the first to be amplified through loudspeakers so the entire crowd could hear it.

Mrs. Harding kept a little red book that listed her and her husband's enemies.

Harding was very fond of his dog, Laddie Boy. For one birthday, Laddie Boy had a party with a cake made of layers of dog biscuits and icing.

President Harding kept a pen of turkeys at the White House.

During Harding's administration, the first presidential speechwriter was hired.

Harding enjoyed poker and gambling. He played the stock market under the name Walter Ferguson.

Although Harding looked calm, he suffered serious breakdowns during stressful times. He suffered his first nervous breakdown at 22 and went to a sanitarium for several weeks.

Calvin Coolidge
(1923-1929)

Coolidge was the only president born on Independence Day. His birth name was John Calvin Coolidge Jr.

President Calvin Coolidge, whose first cabinet meeting lasted 15 minutes, had a reputation for never wasting a penny or a word. Many people even called him Silent Cal.

On his first day in the White House, Coolidge was so lonely that he called the same friend in Boston five times.

Coolidge used petroleum jelly to slick his hair.

Coolidge could play the harmonica, sew a quilt, and doctor a sick maple tree.

The president relaxed by riding a mechanical bucking horse that bounced him up and down. He also enjoyed golfing, fishing, and trapshooting.

One White House cook quit because the president was so cheap. The last straw was when he could not be convinced that it took six hams to feed 60 people at a state dinner.

President Coolidge checked all of his wife's bills to make sure she wasn't spending too much money.

President Coolidge loved animals. His many pets included a raccoon that he walked on a leash and a dog named Paul Pry.

The White House staff called Mrs. Coolidge "Sunshine." They called the president "Little Fellow" behind his back.

In 1923, Coolidge was the first person to light the national Christmas tree. He officially declared Christmas Eve a holiday in 1928.

Coolidge is the only president to have his face put on a U.S. coin while still living. He was on the 1926 half-dollar, which marked 150 years of independence for the United States.

Herbert Hoover
(1874–1933)

President Herbert Hoover's son Allan had two pet alligators, which sometimes wandered around the White House.

Hoover was the first president born west of the Mississippi River. He was born in Iowa.

Hoover's wife, Lou, spoke five languages fluently. Hoover and Lou often spoke Chinese when they didn't want the White House staff to know what they were saying.

President Hoover was the first millionaire to be president. He was a successful engineer before going into politics. He was a millionaire by the time he was 40.

Hoover never accepted his salary as president. He spent his own money on entertaining.

Hoover was the first president to have a telephone. He had one installed on his desk in his office.

In 1931, "The Star-Spangled Banner" became the official United States national anthem under Herbert Hoover. The country did not have a national anthem before then.

Hoover wrote several books after leaving the presidency. He was the first president to write a book about another president, Woodrow Wilson.

Hoover was the first person to use the term "depression" when referring to the economy, which fell into terrible times during his presidency.

Going into the White House, Hoover was a record-setter. He had the largest majority of electoral votes of any candidate up to that time. Leaving the White House, he was also a record-setter. He lost by a new record margin.

Franklin D. Roosevelt
(1933-1945)

At the opening of the New York World's Fair in 1939, Franklin Delano Roosevelt became the first president to appear on television.

In 1905, Roosevelt married his fifth cousin, Eleanor Roosevelt. At the wedding, the president of the United States, Theodore Roosevelt—Eleanor's uncle—gave away the bride.

Roosevelt ran for and was elected to four presidential terms. He was president for 4,422 days. After Roosevelt's presidency ended, the 23rd Amendment was passed. It limits all presidents to two terms in office.

For his entire presidency, Roosevelt could not walk a step without the aid of braces and crutches. He had been paralyzed from the waist down as a result of polio since 1921. Although his legs were paralyzed, Roosevelt traveled more than any president before him.

The informal reports that FDR read to the American people were called "Fireside Chats." However, the fireplace that Roosevelt sat near while giving these reports didn't work.

During his presidency, FDR held a record 998 news conferences. He had a lot to discuss with the American people being that he was president through the Great Depression and World War II (1939-1945).

Franklin D. Roosevelt appointed the first woman cabinet member, Frances Perkins, as secretary of labor.

FDR was the first president to fly in an airplane while in office.

FDR had "Stolen from the White House" imprinted on White House matchbooks.

In 1946, Roosevelt's face was put on the U.S. dime.

FDR was related by blood or by marriage to 11 other presidents: John Adams, John Quincy Adams, Ulysses S. Grant, William Henry Harrison, Benjamin Harrison, James Madison, Theodore Roosevelt, William Taft, John Taylor, Martin Van Buren, and George Washington.

Harry S. Truman
(1945-1953)

Harry Truman's full middle name was "S"—with no period after it. His parents couldn't agree on a middle name, so they decided the initial was a good compromise.

As a boy, Truman got up at 5 a.m. to practice the piano for two hours before school started. As an adult, Truman got up around 5:30 a.m. and walked 2 miles (3.2 km) every day.

By age 14, Truman had read every book in the Independence, Missouri, public library.

Truman was the only president who never attended college.

When Truman ran for re-election in 1948, everyone thought he would lose to Governor Thomas Dewey of New York. In fact, the *Chicago Daily Tribune* even printed the headline: Dewey Defeats Truman. After Truman won, he took a picture holding that newspaper and smiling.

Truman coined the phrase, "If you can't stand the heat, get out of the kitchen."

Before his 87th birthday, former president Truman refused Congress' offer to bestow on him the Congressional Medal of Honor. He felt he had done nothing to deserve it.

16

Dwight D. Eisenhower
(1953-1961)

Dwight D. Eisenhower introduced helicopters to the White House for short presidential trips.

In high school, Eisenhower was in the same class as his brother Edgar. Their high school yearbook wrongly predicted that Edgar would grow up to be president. It said that Dwight would grow up to be a history professor.

President Eisenhower was the first president to appear on color television.

Eisenhower became the first chief executive to celebrate his 70th birthday in the White House.

Ike, as he was called by his friends and admirers, liked to cook. He had a kitchen put in on the third floor of the White House in the family quarters.

The only president to see action in both World Wars was Eisenhower.

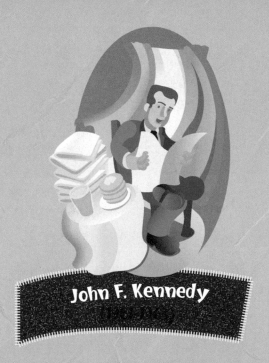

John F. Kennedy
(1961–1963)

Kennedy could read almost 2,000 words a minute with almost total understanding. He would read four newspapers every morning in 15 minutes. He was able to discuss in detail the articles he read in each of them.

Kennedy was the first president born in the 20th century. His wife, Jacqueline, was the first first lady born in the 20th century.

Kennedy's left leg was shorter than his right leg by almost 1 inch (2.5 cm).

As a boy, John Kennedy was often ill. In college, he injured his back in football practice. In 1954, after back surgery, Kennedy was so ill that he was given his last rites. Later, as president, he was known for his vigor and for his physical fitness programs.

During his recuperation from back surgery in 1954, Kennedy began working on the book *Profiles in Courage*. It was published in 1956, became a best seller, and won a Pulitzer Prize.

John F. Kennedy, the first Roman Catholic president, had trouble finding a priest who could hear his confession without recognizing his voice.

Kennedy was the youngest man ever elected president. Theodore Roosevelt was a few months younger when he took office. However, Roosevelt became president after a preceding president had died in office, not by election.

The Kennedy family hated television. They had all the TV sets removed from the White House. But when their daughter Caroline cried to see "Lassie," they had to bring one set back.

While Kennedy was president, he called his father every day.

Lyndon B. Johnson
(1903–1969)

President Johnson had a Texas barbecue on the roof of the White House. He served steaks, baked potatoes, corn pudding, and pecan pie.

Johnson's parents took three months to pick a name for him.

In his first-grade class, Lyndon B. Johnson was already boasting that he would one day be the president of the United States.

Sometimes the president called the press on a moment's notice and had them run along to keep up with his brisk pace as he walked. These instant conferences were referred to as "walkie-talkies."

President Johnson turned out every light in the White House that wasn't absolutely necessary. He even turned out lights as he left rooms. Many staff members who left an office to go to the bathroom returned to find their offices dark. Others complained of bumping into each other along the dark hallways.

Johnson bought his wife's wedding ring for $2.50 at Sears.

The initials LBJ were important to the Johnson family. Every person had them: Lyndon Baines Johnson, Lady Bird Johnson, Lynda Bird Johnson, Luci Baines Johnson, and Little Beagle Johnson (the family dog).

Until Johnson had a severe heart attack at the age of 47, he smoked three packs of cigarettes a day.

NEWS

Richard M. Nixon
(1969-1974)

Richard Nixon has been on the cover of *Time* magazine more than any other person. He holds the record at 56.

The first president 18-year-olds could vote for was Nixon. The 26th Amendment, changing the voting age from 21 to 18, was ratified in 1971.

Nixon combed his hair back to cover a scar.

Because his beard grew in so fast, Nixon had to shave two or three times a day to appear clean-shaven during his political campaigns.

Nixon was allergic to one thing: wool.

One of Richard Nixon's favorite dishes was meatloaf.

On March 24, 1970, Nixon signed a law to ban the advertising of cigarettes on TV and radio.

Nixon was the first president to visit all 50 states while in office.

President Nixon's daughter Tricia was the first person to have an outdoor wedding at the White House. She was married in the Rose Garden in June 1971.

On August 9, 1974, Richard Nixon resigned from the presidency. Evidence that the president had been involved in covering up a burglary by his campaign staff during the campaign of 1972 was mounting. Impeachment proceedings had already begun as a result of the evidence. Nixon is the only president to have resigned from office.

Gerald R. Ford
(1974-1977)

On the day of his wedding, Gerald Ford showed up with one brown shoe and one black.

Until he was 16, Gerald Ford did not know that he was adopted by his father. Ford was born Leslie Lynch King Jr. When he was two weeks old, his parents divorced, and his mother later married Gerald Rudolph Ford, who legally adopted the boy and gave him his own name. The secret was kept from the future president until his high school years, when his birth father told him the truth.

Ford won the "most popular high school senior" contest in his hometown of Grand Rapids, Michigan. The prize was a trip to Washington, D.C.

During his senior year, Ford was named the Most Valuable Player for the University of Michigan football team. He received offers from the Green Bay Packers and the Detroit Lions but declined. He took an assistant football coaching job at Yale, where he later studied law.

Ford once worked as a male model. He appeared in *Look* magazine in an ad for a Vermont ski resort.

Ford was the first vice president to be appointed by a president under the 25th Amendment. He is also the only president who was never elected as president or vice president.

President Ford's favorite lunch was cottage cheese smothered in ketchup. He also enjoyed eating raw onions.

Ford liked to jog, sail, ski, swim, and golf. While playing golf, he once hit a ball that injured a spectator.

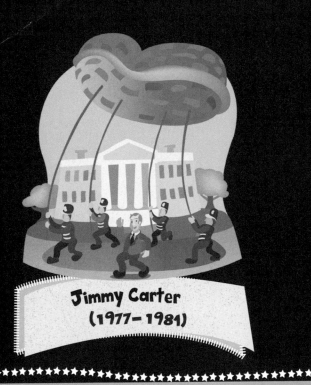

Jimmy Carter
(1977–1981)

Jimmy Carter, the first deep southerner elected president after the Civil War (1861-1865), was a peanut farmer in Plains, Georgia. As part of his Inauguration Day parade, a giant air-filled peanut balloon was floated down Pennsylvania Avenue.

A group from Carter's hometown in Georgia hired its own train, called the "Peanut Special," to go to the inauguration. On the trip to Washington, D.C., the group ate 275 pounds (124 kg) of peanuts.

When he was 12, Carter began to write letters to people who might recommend him as a candidate for the U. S. Naval Academy. Afraid that his flat feet would eliminate him from consideration, he stood on Coke bottles and rolled back and forth to strengthen his arches.

As a young naval officer, Carter suffered from seasickness. When he had to stand watch, he carried along a bucket.

President Carter was the first chief executive to walk from the Capitol to the White House after being sworn into office.

Carter was the first president to insist that people call him by his nickname. His real name is James Earl Carter, but he preferred Jimmy.

Jimmy Carter was the first president to run a TV talk show. Called "Ask Mr. Carter," it was on for two hours, during which time viewers called in with questions or advice for the president. Nine million people made phone calls, but only 42 of them actually got through.

Carter was a speed-reader. He could read 2,000 words per minute and still understand nearly all of what he read.

Ronald Reagan
(1911-2004)

President Reagan always had jelly beans available at Cabinet meetings.

Just two weeks shy of turning 70, Ronald Reagan was the oldest man to be inaugurated president of the United States. He set a new record when he was re-elected at 73.

On March 30, 1981, Reagan became the first president to survive an assassination attempt. As he was being wheeled into the operating room, he looked up at the surgeons and said, "I hope you're all Republicans."

Until Reagan, every president who was elected in a year that ended in zero died in office. This was called the "zero jinx," and Reagan barely escaped it.

Sandra Day O'Connor, the first woman to be on the U.S. Supreme Court, was appointed by Reagan.

Ronald Reagan was the first president to have been divorced. Nancy Reagan was his second wife.

Ronald Reagan was once a star in Hollywood movies. He appeared in more than 50 films, ranging from the serious drama "King's Row" to the comedy "Bedtime for Bonzo," which co-starred a chimp.

George H. W. Bush
(1989-1993)

When President George Bush said he liked pork rinds, the White House was filled with barrels of them sent by well-meaning people.

Bush upset broccoli growers when he banned the vegetable from the White House. He said his mother made him eat the stuff when he was a boy, but now that he was president he didn't have to eat it anymore.

Bush was the first vice president still in office to be elected to the presidency in 153 years, since Martin Van Buren's election in 1836.

George Herbert Walker Bush was the first president to have two middle names.

Bush was the first president to have a birthday in June.

In 1943, at the age of 19, Bush became the youngest pilot in the Navy.

Bush is related to Benedict Arnold, Marilyn Monroe, and Winston Churchill. He is also related to Presidents Franklin Pierce, Abraham Lincoln, Theodore Roosevelt, and Gerald Ford. President George W. Bush is his son.

First lady Barbara Bush's great-great-great uncle was President Franklin Pierce. He served from 1855 to 1857.

Barbara Bush refused to do three things if her husband was elected president: dye her hair, lose weight, or change her wardrobe.

William J. Clinton
(1993-2001)

In high school, President Clinton played saxophone in a jazz trio. The musicians wore dark glasses on stage and called themselves "The Three Kings." However, other people called them "Three Blind Mice" because of the sunglasses.

Clinton's full name at birth was William Jefferson Blythe IV. His father, William Jefferson Blythe III, died three months before he was born. When President Clinton was 4, his mother married Roger Clinton. Years later, Bill changed his last name to Clinton.

As a child, Bill Clinton's nickname was "Bubba."

When Bill Clinton was in high school, he shook hands with President John F. Kennedy. Clinton later said that meeting Kennedy inspired him to go into politics.

At 32, Clinton was the youngest governor ever to be elected in Arkansas.

Clinton was the first president from the "baby boomer" generation born after World War II (1939-1945).

Clinton suffers from chronic laryngitis.

Clinton was the second president (Andrew Johnson was the first) to be impeached by the House of Representatives. The senate voted to allow Clinton to keep his job.

When her husband had completed his term, Hillary Rodham Clinton became the first first lady elected to the U.S. Senate. She was also the first first lady who was a lawyer.

(2001-2009)

George W. Bush is the first president who has run a marathon. He finished the 1993 Houston Marathon in a time of 3 hours, 44 minutes, and 52 seconds.

The son of the first president Bush, George W. Bush served as governor of Texas. He considers himself a Texan, but he was born in New England.

Bush majored in history at Yale. Like his father, Bush was a member of the secretive Skull and Bones group at Yale.

Bush was a cheerleader at Yale University. He also played baseball and rugby there.

Bush is the first president to have a Master of Business Administration (MBA). He graduated from Harvard Business School in 1975.

Bush applied for law school but did not get accepted.

Bush is the first president to have owned a sports team. He bought the Texas Rangers in 1989 and sold the baseball team in 1994.

Bush married Laura Lane Welch after dating her for just three months.

The Bushes are the first presidential couple to have twins. Barbara and Jenna are fraternal twins born in 1981.

One of Bush's nicknames is "Dubya," which stems from his middle initial. His middle name is Walker, which is his mother's maiden name.

administration—the period of time during which a government holds office

amplified—made louder

assassination—the murder of an important or famous person

cabinet—a group of officials who give advice to the president

chauffeur—a person whose work it is to drive another person around

chief justice—the head judge of a court of justice

dyslexia—a learning disability that is usually marked by problems in reading, spelling, and writing

elected—chosen by a vote

generation—a group of people born around the same time

governor—the person elected to be the head of government of a state

impeach—to bring formal charges of unlawful conduct against a public official

inauguration—the ceremony of putting a person in office

paralyzed—unable to move or feel a part of the body

press conference—an interview given by a public figure to news reporters

resign—to give up a job, position, or office

sanitarium—an place for the care and treatment of people recovering from illness

stock market—a place where the buying and selling of stocks is held

succeeding—coming after and taking the place of, such as when a vice president replaces a president who has died

Index

Kennedy, John F., 18–19, 33
"King's Row" (movie), 29

Laddie Boy (dog), 9
Lincoln, Abraham, 31
Look magazine, 25

Madison, James, 15
military service, 26, 27, 31
Monroe, Marilyn, 31
movies, 29

names, 6, 9, 10, 16, 20, 24, 27,
 31, 32, 35
national anthem, 13
nicknames, 10, 11, 27, 33, 35
Nixon, Richard, 22–23
Nixon, Tricia, 23
Nobel Peace Prize, 7

O'Connor, Sandra Day, 29

Panama Canal, 4
Paul Pry (dog), 11
"Peanut Special" (train), 26
Perkins, Frances, 15
Pierce, Franklin, 31
polio, 14
press conferences, 5, 7, 15, 21
Princeton University, 7
Profiles in Courage (John F.
 Kennedy), 19
Pulitzer Prize, 19

Reagan, Nancy, 29
Reagan, Ronald, 28–29
resignations, 23
Roosevelt, Eleanor, 14
Roosevelt, Franklin D., 14–15
Roosevelt, Theodore, 4, 14, 15,
 19, 31

salaries, 13
Skull and Bones group, 34
speechwriters, 9
speed-reading, 18, 27
sports, 5, 7, 8, 11, 25, 34, 35
Supreme Court, 29

Taft, William Howard, 5, 15
Taylor, John, 15
telephones, 13
television, 14, 17, 19, 23, 27
Texas Rangers baseball team, 35
"The Three Kings" (band), 32
Truman, Harry S, 16

Van Buren, Martin, 15, 31
vice presidents, 25, 31

"walkie-talkies," 21
Washington, George, 15
weddings, 14, 23, 24
West Wing, 4
White House, 4, 5, 6, 7, 9, 10, 11,
 13, 12, 15, 17, 19, 20, 21, 23,
 27, 30
Wilson, Edith, 7
Wilson, Ellen, 7
Wilson, Woodrow, 6–7, 13
World War I, 7, 17
World War II, 15, 17, 33

Yale University, 25, 34, 35

"zero jinx," 29

To Learn More

More Books to Read

King, David C. *Have Fun with the Presidents: Activities, Projects, and Fascinating Facts*. San Francisco: Jossey-Bass, 2007.

Pascoe, Elaine. *First Facts About the Presidents*. Woodbridge, Conn.: Blackbirch Press, 1996.

Sobel, Syl. *Presidential Elections and Other Cool Facts*. Hauppauge, N.Y.: Barron's Educational Series, 2001.

On the Web

FactHound offers a safe, fun way to find Web sites related to topics in this book. All of the sites on FactHound have been researched by our staff.

1. Visit *www.facthound.com*
2. Type in this special code: 1404841180
3. Click on the FETCH IT button.

Your trusty FactHound will fetch the best sites for you!

Look for all of the books in the Freaky Facts series:

Ancient Coins Were Shaped Like Hams and Other Freaky Facts About Coins, Bills, and Counterfeiting

Cows Sweat Through Their Noses and Other Freaky Facts About Animal Habits, Characteristics, and Homes

Earth Is Like a Giant Magnet and Other Freaky Facts About Planets, Oceans, and Volcanoes

One President was Born on Independence Day and Other Freaky Facts About the 26th Through 43rd Presidents

Some Porcupines Wrestle and Other Freaky Facts About Animal Antics and Families

Three Presidents Died on the Fourth of July and Other Freaky Facts About the First 25 Presidents

Your Skin Weighs More Than Your Brain and Other Freaky Facts About Your Skin, Skeleton, and Other Body Parts